Tools on the Farm

by Teddy Borth

ABDO
ON THE FARM
Kids

www.abdopublishing.com

Published by Abdo Kids, a division of ABDO, PO Box 398166, Minneapolis, Minnesota 55439.

Copyright © 2015 by Abdo Consulting Group, Inc. International copyrights reserved in all countries. No part of this book may be reproduced in any form without written permission from the publisher.

Printed in the United States of America, North Mankato, Minnesota.

052014

092014

Photo Credits: Shutterstock, Thinkstock, © valeriiaarnaud p.5 / Shutterstock.com

Production Contributors: Teddy Borth, Jennie Forsberg, Grace Hansen

Design Contributors: Candice Keimig, Laura Rask, Dorothy Toth

Library of Congress Control Number: 2013952567

Cataloging-in-Publication Data

Borth, Teddy.

 Tools on the farm / Teddy Borth.

   p. cm. -- (On the farm)

ISBN 978-1-62970-055-7 (lib. bdg.)

Includes bibliographical references and index.

1. Agricultural implements--Juvenile literature. 2. Farm equipment--Juvenile literature. I. Title.

631.3--dc23

             2013952567

Table of Contents

Tools on the Farm

Farmers do some work by hand. Farmers use tools for small jobs.

4

Plow

A plow gets the soil ready for seeds. It can be pulled by horses.

6

Hoe

Hoes can remove weeds. Hoes are used to dig up potatoes.

9

Horse Brush

Farmers brush their horses.

This cleans the horse.

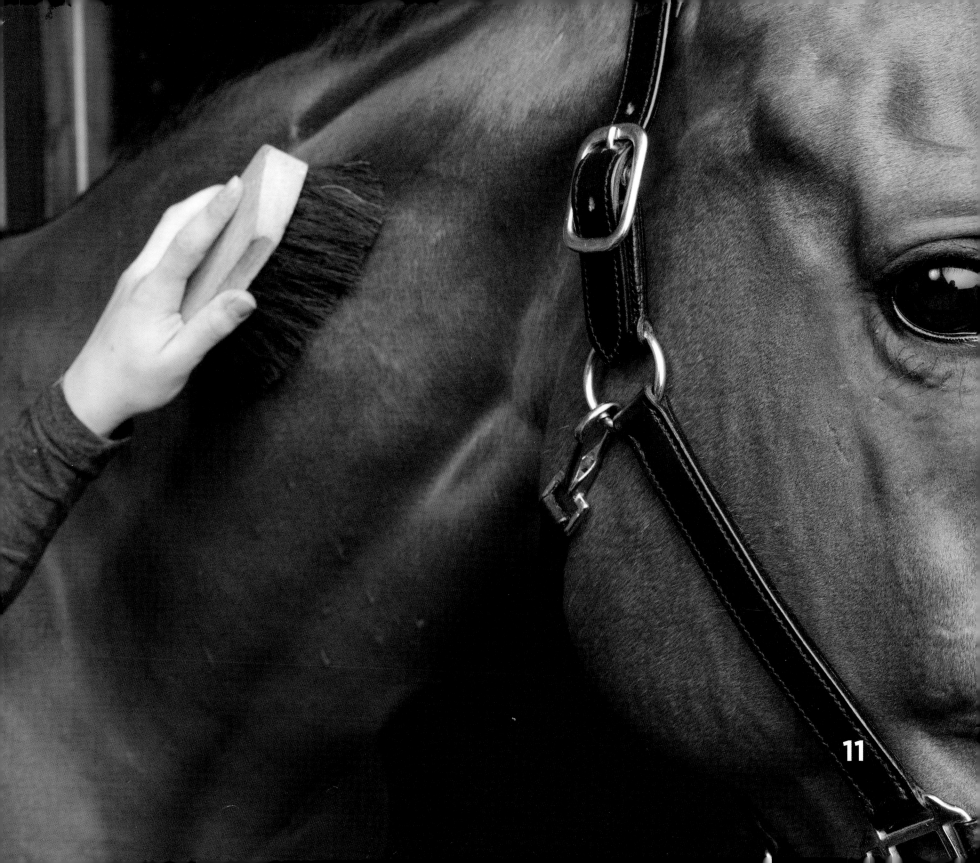

Wheelbarrow

Wheelbarrows carry things.
Most wheelbarrows have
one wheel.

12

13

Pitchfork

Pitchforks are used to lift hay and straw. They have long handles.

14

15

Rake

Rakes are used to **collect** hay and straw. This makes pick up easier.

16

17

Shovel

Shovels can dig holes.

Shovels are used for planting.

Shears

Shears are like big scissors.

They cut **wool** from sheep.

20

More Facts

- Some parts of the world use buffalo to pull plows.

- Hoes are believed to be the first tool humans developed after the digging stick. They are still used today!

- The word rake means "to scrape together."

- Professional sheep shearers can shear sheep in under a minute. The world record is 38 seconds.

Glossary

collect – to take from scattered places and bring together.

weed – a wild, unwanted plant.

wool – the soft, curly hair that grows on sheep and other animals.

23

Index

abdokids.com

Use this code to log on to abdokids.com and access crafts, games, videos and more!

Abdo Kids Code:
OTK0557

24